VAST BEAUTY

By

Kathy
Latham

SECOND SIMPLICITY PRESS

Book Design & Layout: Richell Balansag
Cover Illustration: Ula Patoka

ISBN 978-82-693322-0-9

Published by Second Simplicity Press
Oslo, Norway
secondsimplicity.press

Tio Tom
Thank you for the inspiration

KG
Takk for alt

Artists, teachers, students
Thank you for being you

VAST BEAUTY

I guess this is it
You have to start somewhere, right?
So let's begin now

When we transform, the old us
Dies so we can live again

When nothing else works
Inspire me to inspire you
When you breathe, I'll breathe

With days like this, speak
To the part of me that knows
And knows how to live

Something good is worth
Finding the strength to get through
All that you go through

Effort sacrifice patience
Elevated into art

Don't panic, steady
The light shows us the shadow
So we all can heal

Raindrops, reminders
Simplicity holds treasures
The jewels of truth

Quality of light
Beyond words and images
A dusky white gold

We've all got bridges
to cross between who we are
and the self of dreams

Rise, city of dreams
The magic in your buildings
Brought forth by sunset

Sometimes, the city lives you.

This is where I come from,
But it's not where I am going

Time is the greatest
Gift because we show up for
Love in the present

I think of you when
Our paths meet and it reminds
Me that there is more

I wrote this for you
So you could write a poem
About art and love

Tell me about courage, light
The subtle magic of life

I wrote this for you
So you could see who you are
Reflected in words

The mysterious
World of the interior
We contain oceans

Don't assume he knows
Where the tide is taking you
Tell him how you feel

It needed to end
The distance between us, far
Too great to abide

Wounds healed, I am free
I no longer feel the need
To be loved by you

For I am lit from within
My heart overflows with love

After the sun sets
Think of me when I'm not there
Remember the warmth

The space between us contains
The words we left unspoken

When we are apart
Our prayers and sweet affection
Resound silently

After all these years
I haven't forgotten why
I love you so. Home.

In this time with you
I have almost forgotten
Why I need to leave.

When thoughts go round and round,
You're in your mind.
That's obsession.
When the mind is still and the heart is calm,
You're in love.
Love is expansive.
Obsession is stifling.
How do you choose love?
Go to the places within that you don't want to go.
See what is there.
Give it space.
Have compassion.
Let it dissipate.
Feel the real you.
Believe in that.
And be open to the peace that opens to love.

I surrender, love
I can't chase you forever
Will you come find me?

In the sweetness and
struggle of everyday: Love
Is waiting for us

How does it feel now?
It's warm and rainy, peaceful
Sounds of city streets

Warm on the inside
Is constant on the outside
The inner fire burns

Vastness in harbor
Reflects the width of our dreams
Hazy, expansive

Awaken to frost
Fog on the window, the lake
The full moon sunrise

Thoughtful urban plans
Create languid cityscapes
Such a joy, breathless

Oh traffic calming
Your care for pedestrians
Brightens my evening

Streets like currents
Moving us moving through us
We dance, we walk

Streets like rivers
Carrying us to the shores of our imagination
The oceans that are us

Streets like canyons
Carved by hands before us
Providing the structure, guiding us through

Streets like archives
Paved with footsteps, walking we merge
Into the dancing sea of humanity

After the rainstorm
Someone sat on this bench before me
And it is dry enough to sit
And now slowly,
the park begins to fill with people again

I like the soundcurrent here –
Like the NY of my childhood
The sounds of children playing,
jubilant, chaotic. Playground sounds.
The bounces from nearby ballgames,
reverberating, resounding.
Adults socializing, out loud or
simply by being present, here, on benches.

Soft traffic passes, city life flows.

And the warm summer breeze on my skin
pulses with the pulse of the city.

We sit, enjoying the dusk,
before the night dawns and calls us home.

On a dark corner
The amber flame of streetlights
Says open your eyes

Lenox nine pm
Still save for rustling leaves, wind
Church bells, passing cars

There is a woman.
Painting murals in the sky.
She is not a man.

(The painting heroine)

Here is a man who knows
how to flow with the subtlety of a woman
He provides her with support
- not because she is weak -
to champion her strength
He sees her beauty
- not as something to be consumed or exploited -
as a power to be cherished and elevated
This is the play of the masculine and the feminine
More exquisite than the everyday
Something to aspire to

Wisdom of mailbox
Teaches internal hygiene
Free your emotions

Reading is rad folks
Bear with a pink heart's advice:
Find some joy in books

Love me like we are
In a novela, or not
Maybe less drama

In dreams discover
If it's love that awakens
Or dulls you to sleep

Hidden harmonies
In details of the city
Subtle street wisdom

Hearts behind shutters
If you don't let the light out
You can't let it in

Love is louder than
The stories we tell ourselves
Of we're not worth it

When every heartbeat
Leads you to a golden place
All actions further

Dwelling in infinite space
Love is love is love is love

We've escaped, darling
From the dullness of that world
Let's walk toward the sea

Beings from a brighter place
Live in sunshine of their own

Sometimes its basic
Extend your hands and connect
Just love, its ok

Sometimes when we love
Our presence brings presence to
Our surroundings

Love is the answer
Love is always the answer
Love is what is real

The only magic
I still believe in is love
Love is infinite

Love, the greatest mystery
Love, in spacious purity

The only magic
That matters to me: melt in
Your infinity

Our hands are precious
As extensions of our heart
Give love accept love

In space beyond sound
The poetry of the heart
Flows, ever present

In the void, there is
Space for us
In the cathedral of silence
All lives

Flow: when you empty
You are filled, when you let go
You know who you are

The body is the space to
Which the happening happens

Practice is freedom
If you change the colors change
More light more vision

It's as if there are new trees here
From some enchanted far away forest
Like the city of the everyday
Has been overlaid with a world more magical
Or the depth and essence concealed
Has had it's cover lifted away
Or different things to notice
Have been highlighted and lit up
Like the light glowing green through the branches
Shining ethereal toward the lush interior

Flowers at my feet
And coolness of ancient stone
The air smells of herbs

Such a blue this sea
Like a Homerian tale
Painted pines surround

Intersection of
Past and present, timeless cliffs
Verdant foliage

The morning light a pale yellow
Glowing off building facades
Embraced by the greenery
made greener by the week's rain
The tulips haunt with dots of color

On the shores of life
In the in-between spaces
Awareness begins

The grass dances, watch
Tides of wildflowers woven
Waves across the plains

Because of them I know
That I'm in the right place
For they radiate love

A father and a daughter
Sit across from me, blessed
Their eyes with matching warmth

The soul in his eyes
Reminds me of gems within
He doesn't see me

(A haiku about
A stranger on the subway
Who heals by being)

Desert rose thank you
For living among the thorns
Vast beauty enthroned

Urban rose you shine
Your light hope for the hopeless
Savior of the street

When we find ourselves
We speak the truth within us
Open like the sky

If you forgot your light
Go to the horizon beyond all constructs
Let awareness bloom

With eyes like the sky
You perceive more than is seen
In cool clarity ....

With a heart like the sun
Your lion's gaze
Sparks blazing infinity

Yes winter you're here
Your effortless whiteout scene
Inspires frosty awe

Emerging, the swan
As if from the deepest depths
Of the winter lake

Today is the first day that I felt spring stirring
Not because of the flowers
(maybe because of the birds)
That emergent feeling of ending and new beginning
Subtle muted building intensity
for the new season to burst forth
Now it's only a feeling
The air still chills my skin
But the frost has a different texture
A cleanliness, a template
And now, we wait
For the surge of blossoms

We walk in grace
Because it used to be colder than it is now
And now the afternoon sun
illuminates hazily softly
so that we glow
and the buildings glow
and the colors glow
Warm tones like warm summer in winter
And remembering to listen to the bird songs
reminds me of spring
And the sound of water falling
like a great thaw in the great wilderness

Sakura

Reaching out like feathers in the sky
Constellations of blossoms, voluptuous
In their presence a halo of refinement
Until they drop to the earth like snowfall
Like a healing ointment
That carpets the neighborhood
And sweeps through the streets

If, just for a moment
I have appreciated
The beauty of this tree
In raindrops and full bloom
Then I have experienced
The ecstasy of Spring

Soft rain on soft grass
I sit inside the window
At peace in myself

And now it's summer
Dawning with sweat and freedom
The comforts of heat

The air smells sweet like spring.
Like good memories.
As I step out into the night.

Soon it will be fall
But leaves haven't fallen yet
Enjoy your summer

Fall Summer, Lullwater Boathouse

A bridge for people
A bridge to let the swans through
Bridge to other worlds?

Signets gliding in
Making trails through algae blooms
Seafoam patina

There at the center
One swan plays in a fountain
Filtered oasis

The trees shine with rust
Just barely touched by autumn
Vibrating, alive

The lake like still grass
Lullwater lulls me to sleep
Blanketed by sun

Dynamic motion
As I walk into autumn,
Leaves fall around me

Spring-Fall

The leaves fall from the trees
like blossoms do in spring
A magical descent
Enchanting the earth with color
The flowers die for the leaves
The leaves die for the flowers
Which is richer?
In winter, branches wear garments of silent snow
In summer, they are illuminated
by fireflies and body heat
What if you combined them all together?
That's what this autumn day feels like.

Last fire on branches
Stately pines, moss green backdrop
Leafy flames, sunset

Star shaped leaves, the last
Almost a winter tree now
Yet autumn persists

A dance between the seasons,
the sky and the earth.

Snowflakes, spring blossoms
and falling leaves.

I am held by your
Cycles, the tides that take me
In and out of life

In my heart I know
What is right for me, if I
Listen, I am truth

Forget about wanting
To be something you're not
Embrace the gift you are

In love is a key
That unlocks all prejudice
And frees you to live

Generosity
Is the doorway to true wealth
The nectar of life

Work on yourself
Work on the collective
Work on us
Work on love
Work on forgiveness
Work on hope
Work on being awake
That work is art
That work is consciousness
That work is living

Butterfly heralds
The light of transformation
Chrysalis of truth

Trust in the process, it says
As it flies toward the sun

Ballfields, lounging lawns
Seasoned with seasons, lifetimes
Luminescent grass

Go back to the start
It begins where you are and
The spaces you're not

Sometimes golden is
Shiny and bright. Sometimes it
Lives in subtlety.

Raven caws, he knows
That what lies beneath the one
Underlies the all

Dove in the morning
Flies up to a branch
And then it is gone

If the wind whispers
Listen, it might inspire you
Might harbor wisdom

Slow progress is powerful
Your efforts are beautiful

Create, even though you're broken
You never know when you'll be healed
Pour it all out
Leave nothing unexpressed
For then maybe, in creating -
the wholeness you seek may emerge
-that under the surface
Everything was perfect all along

Creativity
Flows from exploration of
Source of creation

All we see is grace

When in your presence, that grace

The presence of saints

More than sum of parts
When together, synergy
And subtle magic

What part of you lives
In a cage of your own creation?
What part of you will set yourself free?

Move your body to move your mind.
And let the cosmos move you.

Walking through poetry
Waiting to be written – for
Rich is this evening

Secure in myself
I celebrate others worth
Knowing our beauty

She surrendered to
Something greater, that she
Is also a part of

Lets rewind ourselves
Back to where we were more us
We just had to be

To love is to live
With all your being embrace
Where and who you are

Love means patience and tolerance.
It requires strength
and neutrality.

I am one of us
We're not separate, even if
That appears to be

We are more than us
In communion with hearts of
Those past and present

Clouds have lifted the ocean
And its shores have expanded
Beyond the horizon
Beyond form

The space of poetry
Intersects with the physical world
It's become brighter
Begging you to notice

Will you allow
The dimension of wonder
That exists in the everyday
To surface in your awareness

Cloud tide lifts us
Ocean of dreams rises
Grandeur of the nebulous
Exquisite realms of the unknown

The sky is in bloom
Like flowers in the desert
Born after the rain

Cloud rises like a phoenix
Tendrils sweep the mountain peaks

Why would I be there?
Why would I not be here with
The sunshine and rain?

Reality more joyous
Than the fantasies we play

My strength is your strength
For what use is power if
It doesn't serve all

Patience, the heart says
For when you are in the flow
All of life happens

It takes courage to trust this
And live by your own rhythm

Dial down distraction
Listen to what your Self is
Trying to tell you

The world doesn't want
you to struggle on as a caterpillar
It wants you to become a butterfly

Coast Starlight

Coast starlight rolls in
To a sleepy town, itself
A city on wheels

Past mountains dreaming
The stars have just given way
To emerging dawn

Through valleys of pine
We coast into the sunrise
Dark outlines, rose light

Say yes to the sky
Welcome this gift of morning
The path winds forward ...

Now blue emerges
Raising up the vibrant clouds
Mountains awake, glow

In a flash the sun
Bursts through a gap in the trees
Pours into my eyes

We dance, spiraling
Around the sun as it moves
Between the windows

Dusty fields, Cows graze
Haloed under golden mist
The land illumined …

Lakes and streams reflect
A deeper blue than the sky
Placid, pastoral

Everything we see
Was painted by the sunrise
Before we arrived

Everything we see
Will be erased by nightfall
To renew again

On disembarking
Strange not to be on a train
New city, new land

Gare de Lyon
Amrit vela
Subtle sounds
Hushed voices
Because it's early
And that has a palpable sacredness
An unspoken agreement to respect
The silence of the morning
Now were all assembled on this train
Let's make this journey
Morning light like moonlight
And frost like new snowfall
Sheep like otherworldly creatures
Starkly glowing in the landscape
Spectral clouds hug the earth
Anchored by trees and houses
It's a long time before the sky turns pink
Snow capped mountains and the moon waning above
Mountains of sheer solid greatness
One topped with a cross
Tiny in comparison
To the monolith of stone
Saint Jean de Marieux

Kaleidoscopic
This city view
As I glide over the bridge
If you really focus, it's like flying
The train takes you to heights
Suspended over the river
Suspended between worlds
With a loftiness of vision
Smile at the everyday
Marvel at familiar marvels
And remember the magic of the moment
No matter how many times you pass this way
It's always different

The sleeping city
Awakening one by one
Entering the day

Despierta, rise from
The fog and spirals of sleep
Wake up into you

Courage and humor
On the wall makes me smile and
Reminds me of home

Beyond any filth
That gathers on the surface
We are innocent

Wild hearts, their tendrils
Of greenery embracing
The storied city

The air is dry, love
The in between spaces sharp
Until your exhale

The joy you seek, love
That magic lies within you
Yours to discover

Realizing that
I am you and you are me
The hierarchy drops

If it weighs you down
It's not love, it's something else
Love lifts you higher

And if you're feeling
A little broken, let go
And let love find you

Bingo, when you find
What you have been searching for
All the pieces fit

The past illuminated
Unraveled and rewoven

A prayer for those
Enslaved by their own beliefs
That they may know bliss

If it was perfect, it wouldn't be perfect

Devotion does what needs to be done

Quiet strength applied
Adversities are allies
Teaching courage, grace

The old horizons
Open into space, the past
Finds resolution

Freedom is where I am and where you are
Don't get caught up in attachment
There is always a new moment to embrace

Perfection is where you are and where
I am If we are still enough to see
In our hearts beats the pulse of the universe ....

Bliss is where I am and where you are
Accepting impermanence,
We let go and the world is ours

Paradise is where you are and where I am
Grateful for the present,
Our hearts like ashes in the wind

I want for nothing
Dwelling in the heart, I have
Everything I need

Sweat on the dancefloor
We dance to find the stillness
Silence that is love

From the cathedral within
Know, all is blessed, all is blessed

In your sky, there's no
Need for words or images
Only space and peace

Depth and resonance
Within your heart resounds the
Sound of the cosmos

But how do I live?
He asked, she said:
That's when its
Time to trust yourself

The love in our hearts
Unassailable, rooted
Into the cosmos

I love you where the stars meet the sky

Together we face
Challenges previously
Insurmountable

Train your eyes to see
The love that's in front of you
Everyday magic

Remember,
The same love that flows through me
Flows through you

Sidewalk alchemy
Prayerful concrete portal
Bless your loved ones here

Where you are in life
is where you are in love

The sun in our hearts
Where hidden brilliance resides
Let it out sometimes

Why would you run from your light
For it's just you, it's just you

VAST BEAUTY

If things get sad and
You forgot where your heart is
Look behind the pain

Clouds are part of being alive
We can clear them, live lighter

I am a wild flower
My heart burns for the light of the sun
Falling slowly, into the core of me
So that I may shine and dance

The sun melts into the horizon
Into a pool of lava
Into a forgotten harbor

Where will I be when I wake up?
Will I be in your heart?
Will I be in tomorrow's paradise?

Treat yourself kindly
As you would a cherished one
That's how to love more

Can we love, across
Borders, without conditions,
With inspiration?

In your heart my heart
In your light my light, the bliss
Of being one with you

Melt into the sea
Of devotion, surrender
Dissolve into light

Milton Keynes UK
Ingram Content Group UK Ltd.
UKHW020323031123
431755UK00002B/20